Ghosts of Anchor Bay

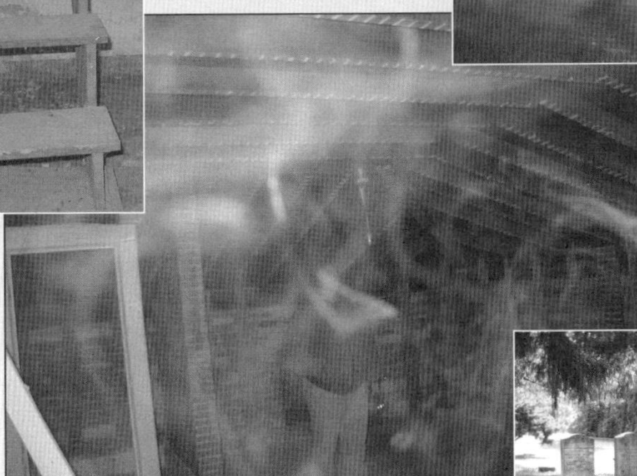

Debi Chestnut
and Linda Sparkman

Schiffer Publishing Ltd®

4880 Lower Valley Road, Atglen, PA 19310 USA

Published by Schiffer Publishing Ltd.
4880 Lower Valley Road
Atglen, PA 19310
Phone: (610) 593-1777; Fax: (610) 593-2002
E-mail: Info@schifferbooks.com

For the largest selection of fine reference books on this and related subjects, please visit our web site at **www.schifferbooks.com**
We are always looking for people to write books on new and related subjects. If you have an idea for a book please contact us at the above address.

This book may be purchased from the publisher.
Include $3.95 for shipping.
Please try your bookstore first.
You may write for a free catalog.

In Europe, Schiffer books are distributed by
Bushwood Books
6 Marksbury Ave.
Kew Gardens
Surrey TW9 4JF England
Phone: 44 (0) 20 8392-8585; Fax: 44 (0) 20 8392-9876
E-mail: info@bushwoodbooks.co.uk
Free postage in the U.K., Europe; air mail at cost.

Library of Congress Control Number: 2005926506

Designed by Mark David Bowyer
Type set in Zapf Chancery Bd BT/Humanist 521 BT

ISBN: 0-7643-2302-4
Printed in China

Dedication

Debi and Linda dedicate this book to the people who have opened their minds and their homes to contribute to this book. Our husbands, for having the patience to put up us. Alice Bliss for her contribution, as well as Lois, Hollie, and Hilari…who know.

There was something awesome in the thought of the solitary mortal standing by the open window and summoning in from the gloom outside the spirits of the nether world.
— Sir Arthur Conan Doyle, British mystery author & physician (1859-1930)

Contents

Foreword

Is it possible those who have passed away can escape the shackles of death and reach beyond the grave to manipulate people and events in the present? Can land, possibly held sacred by a group of people who once occupied it, shun all who dare to trespass? Can a home absorb the emotions from all that occurred between its walls to the point it becomes alive, develops a soul, and takes extreme measures to protect itself? Or, is it simply phantoms from the past roaming the halls to protect secrets long forgotten?

This book will attempt to answer some of these questions.

It is important that you, the reader, be aware of certain facts before you begin your journey.

First, I possess certain abilities that have helped and guided me on this odyssey. I have the gifts of psychometry – the ability to tap into energies to see past events stored in objects and/or land, and the ability to sense the presence of those who have crossed, and in certain circumstances, have them communicate with me.

Linda, after experiencing a deep spiritual journey to get in touch with her Native American roots, discovered, quite by accident, that she was now capable of getting the eerie and mysterious pictures shown throughout this book.

Secondly, you should be aware that some of the investigations into these places and events are still ongoing. I have set forth different possible explanations for what is occurring in these places. These theories are based on what facts are known, and what I've learned through the use of my gifts. It will be up to you to decide what to believe.

Some of the stories included in this book Linda and I did not personally investigate but were simply too good to be left out. These stories come from people who live in the area and experienced them. We've included pictures whenever possible.

There is also a section on orbs, spirits, and light creatures, delving briefly into the theories surrounding these curious oddities. Also included is a section on the strange, and sometimes terrifying, experiences Linda and I encountered while investigating, researching, and writing this book.

Do you have any true ghost stories you'd like to share with us? If so, please contact Debi Chestnut by e-mail at ghostwriter246@hotmail.com
or ghostmist6@yahoo.com.

The locations and names have been changed at the request of the current owners, and the innocent, if any should be found.

Chapter One

Orbs, Spirits, and Light Beings

Orbs can be anywhere, cemeteries, homes, vacant parcels of land, or even at your local supermarket. You can't see them, you can't feel them, but they may be there nonetheless.

When they show up in photographs they generally appear as little balls of white light, although they can also be red, blue, pink, purple, or just about any other color. No one knows for sure how many colors orbs are capable of producing.

If you look closely at some orbs you will notice different patterns within the sphere itself. Like an intricately woven spider web, almost no two are alike. In other orbs there appear to be faces. It's as if someone were looking at you through another dimension or a different place in time. There are a few theories as to what these mysterious balls of light actually are.

Orbs of different shapes in a field.

Some people believe orbs are remote viewers used by aliens from another planet. The theory is that because orbs are very rarely visible with the naked eye, aliens are able to watch the events occurring on Earth virtually undetected.

Followers of this hypothesis feel that through the use of orbs, aliens have discovered not only how to be stealthy in their movements, but also a very economical means of traveling through space and time.

Another theory is that the orbs are actually angelic beings watching over the people on earth. Some believers of this theory feel that the angels come to heal the sick, comfort people in times of need, to act as guardians for soldiers fighting wars, or to protect the weak.

A congregation of orbs.

The most popular theory is that orbs are spirits of the dead in their purest form. It is a belief among some paranormal researchers that spirits, or ghosts, are comprised entirely of energy.

This theory does go a long way in explaining why, when being photographed, more orbs appear in pictures taken with a flash then without – energy reacts to energy.

In fact, while photographing the pictures for this book, Linda and I both heard the crackle of electricity as the light from the flash hit the orbs. Keep in mind, we usually can't see them with our eyes alone, but when the flash goes off the orbs, if present, light up the darkness like a thousand fireflies.

Orbs lighting up the darkness.

In some cases the orbs were moving at the time the picture was taken and look like small comets racing across the landscape.

Orbs in flight.

So the question remains, are orbs remote viewers for aliens? Are they the spirits of those who have passed? Or are they something else, perhaps a natural anomaly? No one really knows for sure, but one thing is certain – they exist.

While orbs react to energy, such as the flash from a camera, spirits, or ghosts, seem able to manipulate different forms of energy such as electricity.

For example, when my father was alive he was extremely fond of all types of electrical gadgets. My husband shared his passion and has wired all the ceiling fans and attached lights with dimmer switches.

Sometimes when I'm writing late at night, the light on my ceiling fan will dim to its lowest point, then brighten, then dim, brighten, and dim yet again and remain there, leaving me sitting in virtual darkness. Well aware it's my father, I will say, "Hi Dad. Can you please turn the light back on?" As soon as the words escape my lips the light goes to its brightest setting. I guess it's just his way of saying he is here, doing well, and keeping an eye on me.

While researching and writing this book, I received several nasty electrical shocks through my keyboard. One or two were strong enough to physically knock me backwards in my chair. I had my husband, who builds computers, thoroughly examine my computer, the wiring, and the keyboard. He could find no problem with any of my equipment. Not taking any chances, I bought a new keyboard. A week later, while making some notes for this book I received another shock that made my skin tingle and every hair on my body stand on end.

Linda reports similar events taking place at her house. These occurrences are outlined in further detail elsewhere in this book.

Ghosts or spirits can show themselves in many forms. Some people have reported seeing ghosts in their earthly form, and could swear the person was standing right in front of them. It takes an enormous amount of energy for a spirit or ghost to show itself in this form.

In other cases, an entity can appear as a filmy white fog, or ectoplasmic mist. Sometimes these mists are visible to the naked eye. Most of the time they show up in photographs without anyone being aware of their presence until viewing the pictures.

A ghostly mist looms outside the house on the hill.

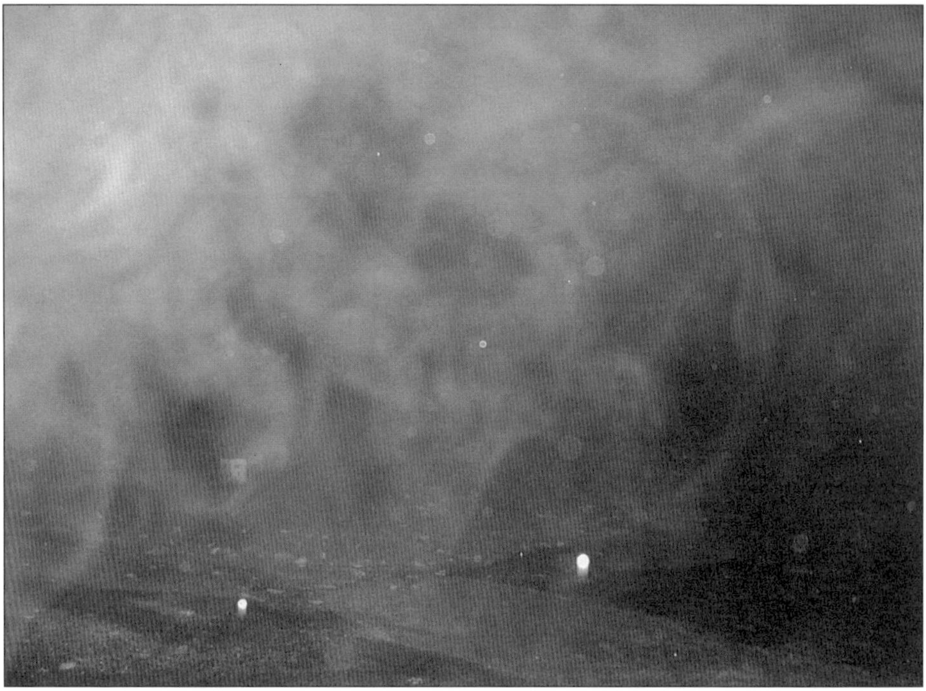

An entity shrouded in a misty fog floats out of Oakwood Cemetery.

There are some people who define ghosts and spirits as two different things. They believe that ghosts are people who have died, but don't realize they are dead, and that spirits realize they have died, have crossed over to the other side, but chosen to return for whatever reason. In other words, ghosts are earthbound and spirits aren't.

Ghosts can be earthbound for a variety of reasons. A person who died in their sleep might literally wake up dead. As funny as this may sound, they honestly wouldn't have any recollection of dying or be aware of their death. They could virtually go for years carrying out their day-to-day routine as they had in life. Imagine their frustration at wanting to communicate with the people around them and not being able to, or having strangers move into the home they still think is theirs.

Another, more complicated reason ghosts might remain earthbound is that they may have unfinished business they are determined to complete.

A murder victim, for example, might remain earthbound to avenge his or hers untimely death. In some cases a ghost might choose to remain here to ensure secrets they so carefully guarded in life remain hidden long after their death.

A spirit, on the other hand, makes a choice to return to their familiar surroundings on earth from time to time. Whether it's to check on the safety and welfare of loved ones, attend a special family event, or to communicate a message, they are not bound to do so, but rather, it's at their option to do so.

When my children were babies, my Great Aunt Louise would check on them from time to time. I always knew when she was there because I'd catch a strong whiff of Chantilly perfume around their cribs. Being allergic to Chantilly perfume, I kept none in the house, but my great aunt wore it every day of her life. I assume it was her way of letting me know she was there.

There's another classification of ghosts, or spirits, known as poltergeists, or "noisy ghosts." They are also sometimes referred to as "mischievous ghosts." No one really knows if they are earthbound ghosts or spirits. Quite frankly, given their behavior, they could be either.

Poltergeists, although rarely seen, are quite active and can be responsible for things that go bump in the night. They have been known to rap on walls and doors, or throw objects across rooms. Lights turning on and off, stereos coming on at all hours of the day or night, are other examples of poltergeist activity.

Although they can put a good scare into you, most ghosts and spirits are generally harmless. However, some can be mean, vindictive, and downright evil.

There have been cases when a ghost or spirit has attacked a living person. Some people who've been a victim of these attacks have been scratched, punched, choked, and have had objects thrown at them.

Little is known about what makes a ghost or spirit evil, but often the answer can be found by delving into the history of the house, or place being haunted. It could be that someone was murdered on the property or there were cases of similar violence. It could also be as simple as a ghost not wanting trespassers in their home.

Whatever the reason, some of these evil ghosts can be hard to get rid of, and in some cases next to impossible, causing people to flee from their homes, never to return.

Throughout history people have come up with different ways to keep evil spirits out of their homes. Some people think that hanging crosses throughout the house works, others have had their house blessed by a member of the clergy. It's also been said that sprinkling sea salt around the outside walls of a house can ward off evil ghosts. There's a theory that, for some reason, an evil ghost will not cross over a line of salt. As far-fetched as it may sound, I've known this to work for some people.

I was involved in one such case. A vengeful ghost was apparently attacking a child. My advice was to make several angels out of any type of material. Paper, cloth, whatever was handy, and as they were making the angels, talk to the child about how God protects children. Once the angels were completed they were instructed to hang one on the outside of the child's bedroom door, and at the foot and head of the bed. Recent contact with the family indicated that since they did this, the attacks on the child have stopped. Go figure.

Whatever means someone employs to rid a place of an evil ghost, all that is important is that it works.

The light creatures, or light beings, as Linda and I call them, are the most mysterious anomalies we've run across in our research. No one is quite sure what they really are. Some people think they are angels, while others think they are creatures from another dimension. Still others attribute them to not being light beings at all, but rather light rods.

A light creature traveling along side us.

It's been suggested they could also be a vortex or portal opening or closing. A vortex or portal is the method some people think orbs, spirits, and other beings travel from their dimension to ours. There is no apparent rhyme or reason to where they show up, or when, they just appear. Linda has photographed them in almost every location we've investigated.

So the debates rage on, yet one thing is certain: orbs, ghosts, spirits, and light beings can be anywhere at anytime, you just have to look and listen.

Chapter Two

The House on the Hill

The townsfolk generally believe the haunting of the house on the hill started on March 24,1881. This may or may not be correct, but that date in the history of New Baltimore, Michigan, is still spoken of today. You see March 24, 1881, is the day Mabel Hatheway died.

At the time of her death she was twenty years, nine months, and twenty-one days old and been married a mere three months to a schoolteacher from Paw Paw, Michigan, named Oren Dunham.

Rumor has it that she was buried in a glass coffin. Her body lays at rest in Oakwood Cemetery. Her grave marker is an ornately carved marble bed.

All that's known of her premature demise is that it was under "mysterious circumstances." An exhaustive search of local and state vital records hasn't turned up a death certificate for her. Not surprising when you consider the entire Hatheway family was, and is, somewhat of an enigma.

Gilbert Hatheway, Mabel's grandfather, came to the New Baltimore area from Massachusetts in the middle 1800s. A merchant by trade, he saw opportunity in this bustling seaside town. With hard work and diligence he became one of the wealthiest citizens in the area. At that time, New Baltimore was a major port on the Great Lakes.

According to known accounts, his son, James, married Evaline and lived in the home with his parents. James, an attorney and merchant, soon amassed his own empire. James and Evaline had one child, Mabel.

The house Gilbert built for his family juts up from the earth in sheer arrogance, defying anyone to desecrate what it perceives to be sacred ground. It stands three stories tall and is adorned in the red brick common to the 1800s.

An angelic figure outside the house on the hill.

Bay windows thrust themselves outward from the first and second stories at the front of the house, giving a cavernous appearance to the weather-beaten wood porch nestled in between them.

The house on the hill.

A substantial cupola, painted blue and encased in windows, sits atop the roof. Towering firs and massive oak trees cast gloomy shadows across the large parcel of land the house commands.

Gilbert Hatheway was elected to the Michigan Senate in 1870, but died during his first term of office in October of 1871. His death certificate lists his cause of death as due to paralysis. Gilbert Hatheway's wife, Abigail, followed him to the grave in March of 1880.

According to Gilbert Hatheway's will, his wife, Abigail, inherited the majority of his estate. Bequeaths were made of $15,000.00 each to Mabel and to the City of New Baltimore to build a school.

James, a ruthless and greedy man, challenged his father's will up to the Michigan Supreme Court where, after two years, he finally lost. New Baltimore got their money and an impressive school was built in Gilbert's honor, aptly named the Hatheway Institute.

James Hatheway, afflicted with severe arthritis, walked with a cane until his illness forced him into a wheelchair and retirement. James suffered a broken neck due to a horrific fall from his wheelchair and died from those injuries in 1887.

James' widow, Evaline, not having a head for money matters soon lost most of the Hatheway fortune due to bad investments. She was forced to sell the house and move in with her sister in another part of the state. Evaline subsequently died in 1923 and is buried in Oakwood Cemetery next to James, and their daughter, Mabel.

Before her death, Evaline had sold the home to a Dr. Virginia Smith, who wanted to turn the home into an insane asylum. However, Dr. Smith was unable to obtain a state license for the asylum and sold the house a year later to Miss. Amanda Tettleson, a spinster from out of town.

Miss Tettleson added a three-story addition onto the rear of the house and transformed the home from a private residence into a successful bed and breakfast known as "The Firs," which operated in the early 1900s. When Miss Tettleson became too elderly to mange the bed and breakfast, she sold the property. Since then ownership of the home has changed hands several times.

Stories of paranormal activity in the house are plentiful, and the house has been dubbed one of the most haunted places in the area.

You can barely see the house for the ghosts.

The tales of the haunting go back to the days of the bed and breakfast. Guests would report hearing footsteps on the stairs. They said the footsteps sounded like someone walking with a cane. Miss Tettleson, when asked about the strange goings on at The Firs, attributed the noise to black walnuts falling from the trees and bouncing off the roof, or to squirrels. (Must have been some mighty big squirrels back in those days to cause such a racket).

Throughout the years many stories have surfaced about the house on the hill. One older couple, who make impeccable witnesses, state that while driving home late one night they pulled into the driveway of the house. The home, at that time, was between owners and vacant. A large lamppost sits by the house, illuminating it at night. Sitting in their car admiring the home, they observed a small boy of maybe five or six run in front of the car from behind a tree. They saw that the boy was dressed in Victorian era clothing and was motioning frantically with his hands for them to get out. The headlights of the car seemed to go right through him. Frightened, the man hurriedly backed the car out of the driveway and didn't stop again until his wife and he were safely in the confines of their own garage.

Research conducted to date hasn't turned up any record of a young boy dying at the home. But, for as wealthy and as prominent as the Hatheway's were, the paper trail is almost non-existent. So the lack of any recorded death of a young boy on the property doesn't necessarily mean one didn't take place.

One of the former owners reported that every night before he went to bed he would put his pocket change on the dresser. When he'd wake up in the morning the change would be scattered all over the floor.

There have also been reports of an entity on the second floor playing with women's hair by either caressing it, swishing it, or if worn in a ponytail, giving it a playful tug.

I attribute the majority of paranormal activity taking place on the second floor to Mabel Hatheway. A well-known psychic in the area, and myself, have both sensed the presence of a young woman about her age on that floor of the home.

Before Linda's friends sold the home, Linda and her husband were regular visitors. Linda's husband was helping the owners do some of the renovations.

On one occasion, Dan, Linda's husband, and Tom, one of the owners, were in basement working on the furnace. No one else was in the house at the time. They both heard footsteps walking around on the first floor and rushed up the stairs to see who was there. They found no one in the house. As they were searching the house, they heard someone banging on something metal in the basement. Rushing down to the basement, they saw no one. As they continued their work, they continued to hear someone walking around the first floor of the house.

A different day, Dan was working alone on the third floor. Someone kept walking up and down the steps. When Dan would go to investigate, no one would be there and upon returning to where he was working he would find that some of his tools were missing. He continued to hear the footsteps and would search the entire house to make sure no one had come in. When he'd once again return to his work, the missing tools would be returned.

Dan also reported feeling cold breezes in the basement and third floor, even on the hottest of summer days. The house was not equipped with air conditioning and the windows were closed. Dan could find no explanation for this event.

On my first visit to the house, the owners at that time were friends of Linda's and were unavailable with keys to let us in, so my initial inspection was limited to the exterior. As I walked up the stairs of the front porch, I felt the flaking dark green paint crumble under my fingers as I clutched the railing. I could sense the sinister presence of a male entity lurking on the other side of the door.

I approached the front door and cautiously reached out my hand to clasp the doorknob. The instant my hand wrapped around the knob, I heard the low throaty growl of a large dog from behind the door. Jerking my hand off the doorknob I called for Linda, who'd been exploring an area to the side of the house. I told her what happened and she said that her friends didn't own a dog. A quick search of the surrounding yards revealed no sign of any animal.

Another thing I noticed was that just about the time the dog growled, the surrounding area became deathly quiet. Considering there are two main streets a hundred feet or so away, it struck me as being unusual.

About a week or so after that, Linda's friends put the house up for sale. I called the realtor to make an appointment to see it, explaining to her that I was researching the original owners. The realtor was anxious to know the history of the house and agreed to meet Linda and me there.

When I walked in the door, I had a vision of a young woman in a white, old-fashioned dress tumble down the stairs like a rag doll. She landed in a heap at the bottom of the stairs and then disappeared. The first floor of the house held nothing else of interest.

As I was climbing the narrow staircase to the second floor, I felt the presence of a young woman. My instincts told me it was the same woman I'd seen tumbling down the stairs a few minutes before.

The main staircase in the house on the hill, complete with resident ghost.

Heading up to the third floor, I became aware of a male entity at the top of the stairs. When I got two or three steps away from the third floor landing, a pair of unseen hands pressed against my shoulders and tried to push me down the stairs. I'd been holding onto the railing tightly, so the attempt by the entity wasn't successful. Immediately I told it to back off and felt him move away from me.

I told Linda what happened and she said her daughter had experienced the same thing, as had the owners of the property.

As we explored the third floor, I found it interesting that the entities wouldn't enter the addition at the rear of the house. This told me that they didn't acknowledge its existence. Therefore the spirits or ghosts in the home were members of the Hatheway family, as they were the last ones to live in the house before the addition.

Linda was taking pictures as I wandered through the house, some of which are included in this book. From the photographs it is apparent that the entity was following me from room to room as I explored the third floor and the cupola.

The entity followed me everywhere. Take note that the mist to my right has formed itself into a wheelchair. James Hatheway, perhaps?

Orbs on the third floor.

We then made our way back down the stairs and into the basement. The basement is divided into several large rooms. To the right of the stairs is a large room containing a furnace and hot water heater. This room is the only room in the basement that has a dirt floor.

When I entered the room my immediate response was that someone was buried in that room. Then I felt an entity filled with a rage and hatred so intense it bordered on pure evil. This feeling became so overwhelming I raced up the basement stairs and outside into the fresh, cool air.

When we left the house, the realtor asked me to conduct a historical tour of the home for the agents in her office that evening. Against my better judgment, I agreed.

That night I met the realtor and approximately fifteen other people at the house. I led them through the house, relating the history as we went along. We eventually ended up on the third floor.

Just as we started our ascent up the short, narrow staircase to the cupola, a large white mist loomed at the top of the stairs. We watched in silence as the mist slowly started to float toward us. We flattened ourselves against the wall as it passed. A few people, too scared to proceed, went scrambling down the stairs and out of the house.

When the mist disappeared somewhere on the third floor, someone asked me what it was. I told them honestly it was probably James Hatheway, explaining that, in life, his favorite place had been the cupola. It's been written that he'd spend hours up there with a pair of binoculars watching his merchant ships come into port at the docks a short distance away. We proceeded with no further incident.

After the cupola we all made our way into the basement. I stood by the basement stairs and let them explore the rooms. I purposely didn't enter the room with the dirt floor, nor did I tell them anything about my earlier experience in the house.

At least ten people approached me separately saying that they believed there was somebody buried in the room with the dirt floor. When I asked what made them think that, all they could say is that it was a "feeling."

The basement of the house on the hill.

Is there a body buried in the basement of the house on the hill? We can only speculate, but my feeling is that there is. Whose? That remains to be seen. The home is once again for sale. It is my hope that someone I know will buy it and let me dig up the floor of that room in the basement to settle the matter once and for all.

Could the young woman I saw toppling down the stairs be Mabel? Assuming it is, did she fall or was she pushed?

The woman I saw came down the stairs backwards, and as limp as a rag doll. Those stairs are quite steep.

She might have hit the back of her head on the edge of the step and died instantly or broken her neck and died a day or two later. The truth is, we will probably never know how mabel died, or if the young woman I saw was her.

For a few weeks after my first visit to the house, I had the same eerie event happen over and over. I would be with some of my friends and in the middle of a conversation, when I would suddenly feel myself drift away. Then I'd have the sensation of flying through the air. The next thing I would see is myself coming in for a landing on the third floor of the house on the hill. I would realize where I was and force myself to go back to my friends. When I came out of this vision, my friends would be calling my name and have scared looks on their faces.

Every time this happened, I wasn't talking about the house or anything else connected with the paranormal. This same event happened at least five to ten times in a one-month period.

The only explanation I have for this is that the entity on the third floor was trying to either communicate something to me, or wanted me there for some unknown reason. If, that is, in fact, it was that being causing this vision, rather than something else all together.

Once, while visiting the family plot in Oakwood Cemetery, located on the outskirts of New Baltimore, I had a vision of Mabel standing by her grave. She seemed very distressed and was pointing to a piece of ground a few feet away. She kept repeating the words, "Something's missing here." She was quite insistent.

The Hatheway family plot. Notice the bed made of marble where Mabel can't rest in peace.

I told Linda what I was seeing, and we carefully looked at the spot Mabel was pointing to. We didn't see anything unusual. Then it hit us; the only graves in the family plot are Mabel and her parents, James and Evaline. Where were Gilbert and Abigail Hatheway?

We drove to city hall and examined the cemetery records. Gilbert and Abigail Hatheway were disinterred and moved to Adrian in 1906! No wonder Mabel was so upset. She didn't know what happened to her grandparents' graves.

Further research at the local library led us to an oral history given by the assistant funeral director at the time. A court order to have the coffins of Gilbert and Abigail

Hatheway exhumed and moved to Adrian, Michigan, was obtained by Isabelle, their daughter.

The account stated that the assistant funeral director was woken up in the middle of the night to dig up the caskets. When the caskets were unearthed, due to a slippage of the straps used to haul the coffins out of the ground, the lids fell open. This document states that the body of Gilbert Hatheway was very well preserved, but his wife's body was nothing but a bag of bones.

He was paid a sum of $50.00 to dig up the graves and stated that was unusual because the normal fee was only $2.00. There is no explanation given for the secrecy surrounding the removal of the caskets in the middle of the night, or why he was paid more money than usual to perform the task.

The coffins were encased in tin by the local tinsmith, and then transported by train to Adrian, where they were reburied in the town cemetery. According to the records in Adrian, the cemetery was moved in 1907 from the middle of town to another cemetery within the city limits, which, just coincidently, happens to also be named Oakwood Cemetery.

On another visit to Mabel's grave, I "saw" her standing pensively beside the mammoth pine tree next to her grave marker. She was wearing a long white dress, and had her left hand clutched to her throat.

As I got out of my car, Mabel looked up at me and asked me what happened to her necklace. I asked her what the necklace looked like and I saw a vision of a delicate gold necklace with intricate silver leaves surrounding a large red stone.

Mabel went on to tell me that she thought the necklace was in her room at the house, and pleaded with me to find it, then she disappeared.

I told Linda about what I'd experienced and a few days later, while inside the house, we literally tore the place apart looking for any type of hiding place a necklace could be, but found nothing. This wasn't surprising since it's highly probable that, if the necklace was left in the house, someone found it long ago.

I'm still searching for the necklace at every antique store and show I visit, but, as of yet, haven't found it.

While doing the research and investigation into this house, I talked to many people about it, including a lot of my friends who wanted me to drive them by the house.

Every time I took one of my friends by the house, the next day they would fall ill. Not serious illnesses mind you, but just sick enough to keep them out of commission for about a week. This phenomena distresses me greatly and I've stopped taking people anywhere near the house for fear that the illnesses will become more severe.

As for the house on the hill, I can't help but feel as though it has taken on a life of its own, apart from the phantoms that still roam its halls. No matter what room you're in, there's a feeling of being watched.

It's as if the house is still protecting the family that once lived within it, and is ready to pounce if you get too close to unraveling the mysteries and discovering the secrets that are, after all these years, safely tucked away within its walls.

Even though the house has fallen into a state of major disrepair, and is in desperate need of renovation, it stands as regal and stately as ever, watching the passage of time from the top of the hill.

Chapter Three

25 Mile Road

Many people associate a haunting with some type of building, home, or, in some cases, a cemetery. Images of a spooky house on a dark, gloomy street, or eerie, mystical apparitions performing a macabre dance among tombstones in a cemetery, come to mind.

However, sometimes a parcel of land, or a particular road can contain paranormal phenomena. A quarter-mile stretch of 25 Mile Road is one such example.

At first glance the potholed dirt road appears to be quite similar to the many other rural streets that stretch for miles through Northern Macomb County.

The tall trees and sparse underbrush lining this small patch of 25 Mile Road reveal nothing out of the ordinary, yet something feels out of kilter with the rest of the landscape.

When I slowly drive through this area I feel as if there are a lot of people walking along side the car peering in at me. Sometimes the closeness is unbearable, almost claustrophobic, and at other times there is only the feeling of being watched by unseen entities safely concealed behind the trees.

Linda and I have spent a considerable amount of time in the last four years attempting to unravel the mystery of this unimposing section of byway. We've photographed it at different times of the day and night. The photographs, while offering up some clues, do little to explain what is occurring there.

Both of us have spent hours walking through the woods on either side of the street looking for clues to explain the enigma, only to resurface with nothing but a multitude of mosquito bites for our efforts.

We've even gone as far as flagging down motorists who've sped through that patch of road like the devil himself was chasing them. When questioned, they report just feeling "weird" in that area.

Linda swears that once, while driving home, she had a vision of a horse drawn hearse with a coffin on it coming up that section of 25 Mile Road. She said there were a lot of people dressed in black Victorian mourning clothes walking along side it. The coffin was resting in a glass enclosure on the back of the hearse.

Given the close proximity of Oakwood Cemetery, which was in existence during the Victorian Era, what Linda saw goes a long way in explaining what I sense while driving down that street.

It is important to note that what some people consider a "haunting" really isn't a haunting at all. A theory among some paranormal researchers is that a certain event from the past gets stuck in a time warp and keeps replaying itself over and over, like a videotape. This event, while playing itself out, may resemble ghostly activity, but in reality there is no spirit present.

Orbs along the side of the road. They appeared to be following us that night.

Applying this theory to Linda's vision and my experiences on 25 Mile Road, it is possible that a long forgotten funeral procession got caught in a time continuum and has been repeating itself over and over for more than one hundred years.

Pink orbs chasing a light being.

While delving into the local history of the area, we found another possible explanation. According to various historical documents and writings, Macomb County has sometimes been referred to as the place where Native Americans came to bury their dead.

A ghost and orb playing a game of tag!

We also learned that throughout history, warring tribes fought vicious battles on land that subdivisions, stores, farmland, and woodlands now call home.

Many Native American cemeteries and burial mounds have been discovered throughout the county, some dating back to 600-900 B.C. Could there be an undiscovered Native American burial site hidden somewhere in the woods along 25 Mile Road?

While we have found no evidence to support this theory, we can't disprove it either. The land on either side of the street is private property and quite expansive, thereby making any exploratory excavations impractical to say the least.

So for the time being anyway, 25 Mile Road will remain a mystery. We will continue to take photographs and search for clues that will help us explain the phenomena occurring on a little country road in rural America.

Chapter Four

The Mills House

The Mills house is a pre-Civil War home located on the outskirts of New Baltimore, Michigan. The rambling three-story white farmhouse sits on approximately three acres of land complete with an old barn and remnants of various outbuildings.

According to relatives of the original owner, Daniel Mills, the house was once a stop on the Underground Railroad. Evidence of this became abundantly clear when Linda fell through the first floor into a pit-like room. Accessible through what appears to be a dark, claustrophobic closet, located under the main staircase, closer inspection reveals a small set of stairs leading down from the back of the closet. Could this be the room in which the former slaves were hidden?

At the bottom of this virtually invisible staircase lays a room approximately ten feet across and fifteen feet deep. The walls of this room are made of various sizes of fieldstone held in place by either mortar or some other material. On the sand floor sits some type of bench. This bench apparently was used by the slaves to rest until it was time to move to the next stop on their way to freedom.

The secret room under the stairs.

The various owners of this property, most of which are direct descendents of Daniel Mills, have observed many unexplainable events. One woman reports that she lived in the house as a child. She and her sister named one of the old parlors of the house the "Funeral Room." They remember coming down the staircase in the middle of the night to get a drink of water. From the kitchen they saw a dim light coming from one of the rooms.

When they looked into the room they were astonished to see that a large table sat in the middle of the room replacing their furniture. Lying on the table they saw what appeared to be a dead body. The room was also filled with many people dressed in black clothing common to the Victorian Era.

Paralyzed with fear they stood staring at the scene in front of them. Then they noticed that all activity in the room suddenly ceased and the ghostly apparitions were staring at them. Gathering courage they bolted back upstairs to their bedroom. The next morning the room that just a few hours ago had been transformed into a mourning chamber was now returned to normal. This same macabre scene played itself out several times during their childhood.

The girls also report that they saw a beautiful young woman standing in their room one night. She had blonde, shoulder length hair and was holding a candle. She motioned for the girls to follow her, but they were so scared they turned the lights back on and she disappeared.

They also reported hearing footsteps on the staircase almost every night and believe it was children because they could hear them playing on the steps.

One of the girls said that she was sleeping in the bedroom at the top of the stairs and would feel icy cold hands in the middle of her back. Then once she felt a very warm, loving touch on her shoulder. There was no one in the room. After that event, she never felt the cold hands again.

They also smelled a strong odor in one of the bedrooms, but only during the day, never at night when they were sleeping.

The father of these sisters also reported bizarre happenings in his second floor bedroom. On a few occasions he would be awakened during the night to see tiny lights of all different colors swirling like a tornado around the room. Afraid to move, he would lie in bed and watch them until they eventually disappeared as mysteriously as they appeared.

Unable to resist such tempting tales, Linda and I decided to conduct our own investigation of the Mills house. After gaining permission from the owner at that time, we spent a considerable amount of time exploring the home's many rooms.

While the pictures Linda took of the inside revealed little of the home's secrets, the pictures of the outside were a lot more telling.

Orbs abound outside the Mills house. Perhaps a family reunion?

Notice the ghost in the window.

An eerie white figure showed up in several of the pictures peering at us from one of the windows. This apparition can probably be attributed to the mother of one of the former owners who died in the home. To be more specific, she died in the exact room the apparition appeared. Linda and I checked with the former owner and learned that his mother spent hours staring out that very same window into the front yard.

On one occasion Linda and a friend, Karen, went to the house late at night to conduct a little more research. While standing in one of the second floor windows, Karen grabbed Linda's arm and exclaimed that she'd just seen a large white figure run across the front yard of the house. At that very same moment Linda heard a man's voice yelling, "Get out! Get out now!" Not needing any further encouragement, Linda and Karen quickly left the house.

On another visit to the house, Linda and a friend of hers, Marie, found an old book in one of the upstairs bedrooms containing the genealogy of the Mills family. Linda decided to take the book home to make copies and return it to the house a different day. Upon returning to Linda's house, Marie became obsessed with reading it. That night, Linda and Marie returned to the Mills house. As they were walking toward the house, Marie pointed to an upstairs window where Linda and Marie both saw a man with a full beard and mustache. He stood staring down at them. Linda and Marie returned to the car and made a fast exit.

The next day they returned and walked around the house. They looked up to the second floor and once again they saw the same man looking down at them. Linda snapped off a few quick pictures and they returned to the safety of the car and left.

From the time they first observed the man on a Friday until Sunday afternoon Linda and Marie experienced unexplained nausea and generally felt very ill. Coming to the conclusion that removing that book from the home triggered their illness, Linda returned the book to the house. Almost immediately their mysterious ailments vanished.

Over the years the home has fallen into a state of disrepair. In the last few years the house has changed hands at least five times. The current owners, who have no intention of leaving anytime soon, are in the process of restoring the home to its previous glory. Since beginning the renovations, it appears that the paranormal activity has calmed down considerably.

The only complaint the owner has is that a window in one of the upstairs bedrooms constantly opens by itself. It seems no matter how many times they shut and lock it they return a while later to find it unlocked and open.

Perhaps all the spirits wanted was someone to restore the home and lovingly care for it as much as they did when they themselves walked among the living.

Chapter Five

The Albrecht House

The Albrecht house is located in Northern Macomb County on a quiet dirt road. It stands alone completely shrouded by tall trees.

The house by day.

The home is completely abandoned and has fallen into a state of total disrepair. Someone has boarded up the windows on the first floor to prevent trespassers from entering the house.

Our investigation took place before the home was boarded up. While we did not enter the property, we peered through the windows and were dismayed to see that all the personal belongings of the owners still remained inside.

In searching old newspaper and land records, we discovered the last owner of the property was a woman named Lauretta Albrecht who died in the home in 2001. Since her death, many paranormal events have been noted.

One person reports that while walking around the home one day, she took a peek inside the living room window. She saw the apparition of a partial misty body. She only saw arms and the faint outline of a head. The spirit seemed to float across the room and disappear into a wall.

Linda and I went to the property several times to take pictures of the outside. We were at the back of the house and, while Linda was shooting photographs, I was wandering around the yard. I felt someone push me toward the road. I spun around, thinking it was Linda, but no one was behind me, and Linda was about fifty feet away, still taking pictures.

One night while there, we saw an eerie glow coming from the upstairs windows. It seemed to go from room to room. We knew there was nobody in the house, as the house was completely boarded up at that time and there was no sign of forced entry. We continued to watch for about fifteen minutes or so as the light wandered throughout the house, then it disappeared as mysteriously as it had appeared.

On several different excursions to the property Linda and I have felt sudden bursts of an icy breeze, even during the hottest days of summer. We mostly feel these if we approach the house. If we keep a respectful distance away, we don't seem to be bothered.

We have recently learned that Lauretta Albrecht didn't have any close relatives, only some nieces and nephews who live out of state. We can't figure out why none of them have come to clear out all of the personal property of their aunt, or put the house up for sale.

While it is our opinion that the home is beyond repair, the property would still have some value. As it stands now, the house, in the recent past has fallen victim to ghost hunters and other groups claiming to be "urban explorers," whatever that means.

We know these people have broken into the home several times and done a tremendous amount of damage to the property. Perhaps this is why Lauretta Albrecht's spirit still roams the home, making feeble attempts to chase out the intruders. No wonder she can't rest in peace. There's no peace to be had.

Chapter Six

Oakwood Cemetery

The exact date Oakwood Cemetery came into existence is as mysterious as some of the events surrounding it. According to records kept by the City of New Baltimore, the cemetery was established around 1870. However, some of the tombstones record dates twenty years or so before that. Some of the markers have been so ravaged by the passage of time and weather they are virtually unreadable and may date back even further.

Our investigation into the cemetery led us on a sometimes-bewildering quest, and most of the time we felt like we were chasing our tails.

We started our search at city hall, and were given a copy of a huge map of the cemetery. It listed Section numbers, grave numbers, and the names of people buried in those graves. It also showed a Potter's Field located on the grounds.

A Potter's Field is a specially designated place in some cemeteries where people who can't afford a funeral are buried, or if the people who died are unknown to anyone.

Armed with our map, we drove to the graveyard to search for Potter's Field, finding it towards the back.

We returned to city hall and asked to see the records of the cemetery. We were handed a large book and began to peruse the entries. We immediately noticed that the map at the front of the book didn't indicate a Potter's Field even existed, yet the map we had distinctly indicated one was there. We also noticed that the entries in the book started in the middle to late 1930s.

We returned the book to the clerk and asked for the book that listed the first hundred years of records for the cemetery, and were told that none existed, and if they did, the city was not in possession of them.

Linda and I then went to the Historical Society to see if they had any information. They didn't, and weren't aware of the Potter's Field.

This whole situation had us confused. Why were there two different maps to the cemetery?

A few weeks later I returned to city hall on another matter, and spoke to a different clerk. I told her about not being able to locate the records for the first hundred years of Oakwood. She asked me to wait a second and disappeared into a back room, returning a few minutes later with a book filled with crumbling pages. The pages had been laminated to prevent further damage. She handed me the book stating that it was the book containing the earliest cemetery records known. I quickly scanned the book and found entries for Potter's Field. After having a copy made of the book, I left.

Still, the mystery remains. How and why are there two maps of the cemetery, why was Potter's Field intentionally left off the newer map, and how can records not be in existence one minute, and appear out of nowhere the next? We can only speculate, as this is one mystery that just won't be solved.

Oakwood Cemetery by day is normally a quiet, peaceful place. A one-lane dirt road winds its way among the massive oak trees and graves. Squirrels scamper around the stone monuments in search of acorns, seeds, and berries. People from the neighboring subdivisions can often be seen walking their dogs or jogging around the grounds.

By night, however, it takes on a different tone. Pictures of the graveyard at night reveal very active patterns of paranormal activity.

Orbs abound and light up the darkness like glittering diamonds when hit with the light from the camera flash. Spirits, in the form of ectoplasm mists, appear seemingly out of nowhere in front of the camera, perhaps as curious about us as we are about them.

Orbs bursting through the gates of the cemetery.

Right:
The Hatheway graves by night.

Orbs, orbs, everywhere!

Most of these spirits seem harmless enough, but on one occasion that wasn't the case. Linda and I were in the cemetery late one night. As we were driving from the back of the burial ground toward the main gates we saw two men closing the gates, shutting us in.

We watched in shocked silence as they walked down the sidewalk along the outside of the cemetery. When they reached a streetlight they simply vanished.

I jumped from the car and raced on foot toward the entrance while Linda followed in the car. With shaking hands I fumbled with the chain holding the gates together. Linda kept an eye out to make sure the men didn't return. After what seemed like an eternity I finally got the chain off and yanked open the gates far enough for Linda to drive out. She stopped the car only long enough for me to jump into it. Shaken, we called it a night.

A ectoplasmic mist greets us at the cemetery gates.

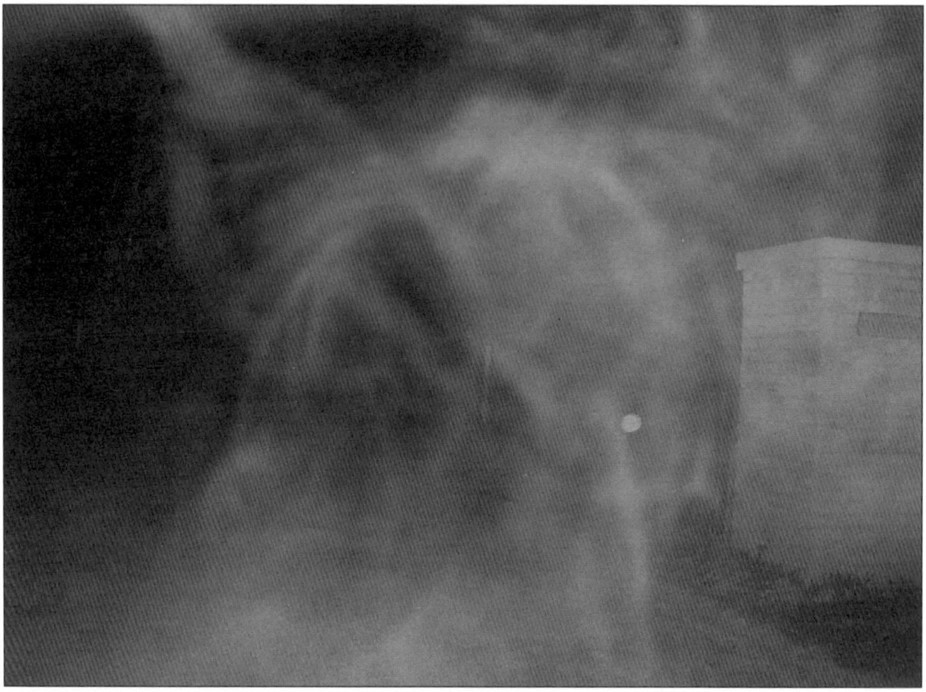

The Guardian of the Gate posing for the camera.

Since that experience, we've consistently had a white mist we call the "Guardian of the Gates" appear in a lot of photographs near the entrance of the cemetery. This apparition, while always appearing in the pictures as a mist, can, and does, take many different shapes. We now park outside the main gates when taking pictures late at night.

During a visit to Oakwood while working on this book, we were surprised to see a wooden cross on Mabel Hatheway's grave. Considering she's been dead well over a hundred years, and no family members remain in this area, it struck us as quite odd.

We photographed the cross, and mused as to how it got there, and, more importantly, who put it there.

About three weeks later, the cross disappeared from the grave. We didn't think too much about it until a couple weeks later when Linda's husband found the cross in one of the flowerbeds in her yard. We have no clue how it got there. If it was done by a spirit trying to send us a message, we don't know what the message is; at least not yet.

Chapter Seven

Linda's Story

In December of 1992, Linda, her husband, and their children moved into the home they still live in today. The house is a two-story colonial built in 1972.

When originally built, the house sat on thirty acres and was a horse farm. The barn burned down with the horses in it. Twenty-six horses died in the fire that was ruled an arson.

Looks like someone followed us home!

A light creature and an entity enjoying the garden.

At times, Linda can still see the horses running the land and hear them braying.

After living in the home for about two weeks, Linda was drawn to Oakwood Cemetery and Mabel Hatheway's grave. She visited the grave often and began having dreams of buying a certain camera. After putting it off for several weeks, the dreams became so persistent that she finally gave in and bought the camera. That's when Linda started getting the pictures you see in this book.

At first, taking these pictures seemed very strange. She'd never experienced anything like this before. Once she became used to getting these pictures, she started experimenting.

Linda went with one of her friends to take pictures one night. She was getting beautiful pictures of huge pink orbs, and orbs that had a pink mist around them and were purple in the center. Her friend was photographing the same scene with her camera, yet nothing was showing up in them. They switched cameras and Linda was still getting the same orb pictures while her friend got nothing.

Then Linda discovered that if she touched the person taking the pictures, they would get the orb pictures also. Was it possible to pass this energy on to another person to enable them to get the pictures Linda was getting?

Why Linda is able to photograph these orbs and such is still a mystery. Sometimes she's woken up in the middle of the night by some unseen force to go out and take pictures. Those could be of her living room or seventy miles away. She never knows where she's going to end up.

While taking them, no matter the time of night, she never feels fear. In fact, Linda feels like she's being protected by something. Linda attributes this to a spiritual journey she took to delve into her Cherokee heritage.

In dreams, or visions, while sleeping, three Native American chiefs visit her. They tell her they are her grandfathers and have waited a long time for her to get here. Then they take her different places.

The first place they took her was to a red clay cave. All the walls sparkled like gold. One of the grandfathers told Linda, "It is here." She didn't think to ask him what he meant because she was in such awe of the beauty surrounding her.

Several times after that, one of the grandfathers will take her part way and she has to complete the journey.

When she gets there, she's standing before tall, bright, white beings. While there, they communicate to her, but upon waking up, she can't remember anything said.

Linda doesn't yet understand the meaning of this journey, but, in time, hopes to be able to. In the meantime, Linda feels the presence of these grandfathers with her all the time.

Around the same time she started being able to take these pictures, strange things began to happen in her home. Linda's daughter would see a beautiful young woman dressed in Victorian clothing upstairs in the hallway. She also saw a little girl of about three in a red dress playing in the same hallway.

Linda's brother-in-law fell ill, and she would spend a lot of time at his house helping to care for him. She would be gone for several days at a time, leaving her husband at home.

Linda's husband was watching television one day when he saw a dark figure walk across the kitchen. Thinking he was seeing things, he ignored it. A few minutes later he once again saw it walk across the kitchen. He got up and went to look around. As he stood there it came back, and walked right past him. He said the figure was about six feet tall, very dark, almost black, and quite solid. He couldn't see through it.

He watched as it walked out of the kitchen and into the dining room. It paced between these two rooms about four times, and appeared to be looking for something or someone. Since Linda was never home when he saw it, it is assumed that this shadow person was looking for her.

Linda has never seen the shadow person herself, nor been able to photograph it. But since her brother-in-law passed away, her husband hasn't seen it since.

One of Linda's friends, Marie, a frequent visitor, often spends several nights at Linda's home. Marie lives quite a distance away, and this arrangement is easier.

Marie says that several times she has heard what sounds like a television. She goes through the house to see if someone is up, or has left the TV on, but every time there's been no one and nothing on. She has also heard the soft murmuring of voices when everyone is sleeping and heard footsteps go up and down the hallway.

Marie also reports seeing a young woman in a long white dress or nightgown walk down the hall and disappear into Linda's bedroom. When she goes to see who it was, no one is there. She's also had the experience of someone touching her shoulder or hair while lying in bed.

One morning Marie woke up before everybody else and went downstairs to make coffee. She took her cup of coffee into the living room and sat down on the sofa. A music box on the fireplace started to play by itself. At the same moment Marie saw a dark figure walk across the room.

Linda and Marie both told me that lights blink on and off, mostly in the living room. They hear people walking up and down the stairs at different times of the day and night.

I personally visit Linda's house quite a bit and every time I try to leave I can't get the front door open. I know it's unlocked because I just walked through it. It feels like someone is holding it shut.

After a few minutes of pulling and tugging, I finally ask whoever it is to let me out. I try the door again and it opens.

On other occasions, the presence won't let people in the house, even their friends.

Some rather disturbing events have also taken place. Every time Linda's daughter is pregnant, someone has pushed her down the staircase. Thank goodness neither the baby nor her daughter has been injured each time this has happened.

With each pregnancy her daughter has been warned by her deceased Grandmother that something is wrong and to go to the hospital. Linda's daughter would only see the top half of her Grandmother's body. On all occasions, when getting to the doctor, emergency C-sections have had to be performed.

While researching this book, Linda has also experienced a multitude of computer problems. The computer is less than a year old. New parts have been replaced but to no avail. The computer problems persist.

Its been rumored that the people Linda's family purchased the home from were involved heavily in the crime world. The entire basement of her house was filled in with sand before the home was sold. Linda has talked to surrounding neighbors, and no one can offer up an explanation for this.

Is it possible that someone is buried under the tons of sand in Linda's basement? Yes, it's possible. If so, could it be this ghost seeking vengeance for his violent death? It certainly would explain some of the events taking place in the home.

Since we've been working on this book, lights seem to go on and off by themselves, especially the one by Linda's computer. Not just that, but light bulbs have exploded on several occasions.

Linda also has reported the sensation of what seems to be an electrical current, or energy, running up through her feet and throughout her body.

The investigation into Linda's home is, and will continue to be, ongoing. We have yet to search land records or other historical writings that might help explain the bizarre phenomena occurring.

Chapter Eight

The Guests Who Never Left

At the time I became associated with the house in Southfield, Michigan, my great aunt occupied it. The house is a typical two-story bungalow with a circular driveway and a large back yard filled with flowers and a giant old apple tree.

The abstract of the property states that Native Americans originally occupied the land before a treaty was signed with the British in 1807. After this time, and up until May 10, 1830, the land was considered to be a United States Territory. Sometime around 1920 the land was subdivided, at which time my Great Grandfather purchased several parcels.

Most of the original house remains intact, although it has been updated periodically. However, until my husband and I sold the property in 1987, the home had never been owned by anyone outside the family.

I first became aware of something being "different" about the house when I was seven or eight years old. Most of the activity at that time seemed to occur on the second floor that was closed off from the main house and used mainly as storage. Sometimes I would be allowed to play up there and was always acutely aware of someone or something watching me.

While playing in the backyard, I would never look up at the second floor window because I knew somebody was standing in the window looking down at me. I could feel their eyes constantly upon me.

Since I was so young, it was very difficult to get an adult to take me seriously. So, I bided my time until I could live in the house and further explore the events taking place there.

There is one incident that sticks out in my mind. I remember as a child playing on the second floor one day. I'd reorganized some things in the east bedroom. That night I was awakened by a sharp slap to the back of my head. I woke with a start to see one of my aunt's slippers falling to the floor at the side of the bed. My aunt lay sleeping peacefully beside me, and was undisturbed.

In order to avoid confusion, I'm breaking down the house into three floors, since each floor of the house had some sort of activity. The basement is a so-called Michigan basement with large old windows on two sides. I don't feel that the basement was haunted, but simply held an event replaying itself over and over. During the early spring and on other rare occasions, my husband and I were always awakened between four and five a.m. by the sound of a heavy metal object being dropped on the basement floor. We'd leap out of bed and rush to the basement only to find nothing out of place.

I told my father about the noise and he said that when my grandfather was farming the land, he used to keep his horse drawn plow suspended from the ceiling of the basement. When he wanted to plow the fields, he would release a rope and allow it to fall on the floor. He'd then hook it up to the horses and have them drag it out the large window to the fields. Thus was solved the mystery of things that go bump in the early morning hours. One thing I learned about living in a haunted house is that a sense of humor is essential!

One of the first incidents in the house occurred the day after I moved in. I'd hung two pictures in the living room, both of which were painted by my Great Grandmother. One picture I hung over the couch, and the other one I hung over the fireplace. The next morning when I got up, the pictures were reversed. No matter how many times I would put the pictures back into their original positions, they would reverse themselves by the next morning.

Frustrated, I called my mother and asked her where the pictures were hung when my Great Grandmother was alive. My Mother told me where they were and I immediately realized I'd reversed them from their original positions. Assuming it was my Great Grandmother changing the pictures, I finally gave up and left them where she wanted them. Sometimes it's just easier to let the spirits have their way.

The main floor of the home consisted of a living room, dining room, kitchen, bathroom, and bedroom. The activity that took place on this floor varied and still is quite a puzzle to me as the activity was never very consistent. I don't even have a label for what it was that occupied this floor of the house. Whatever it was, or whoever it was, I feel it was very powerful.

It would constantly watch me or anyone else that came into the house. You could almost feel its eyes boring into you. Guests in our home would comment about feeling as if they were being watched.

During the times when the presence on the first floor was strongest, my cats would flee from the room like scared rabbits. They couldn't be coaxed back into it until the being went to a different part of the house.

This being, while almost constantly present, would at times make its presence felt more than others. The impressions I picked up from him is that he was basically harmless, but I kept getting a great sense of power from him.

At times I was very afraid of him, but at others he was a comfort. He was often in a playful mood and would turn the kitchen light off and on. Sometimes he would stare at me, and if I ignored him, he would turn the TV off or on and if that didn't work he'd turn the stereo on full blast.

When he displayed this type of behavior I would sit in the living room and talk to him about anything I could think of for anywhere from thirty minutes to an hour. I tried setting ground rules but he very rarely obeyed them. However, when I had my baby he was less likely to turn on the stereo or TV to get attention if the baby was sleeping.

One of my friends was quite terrified of him, and he knew it. Every time she went into the bathroom, he wouldn't let her out. No matter how hard she tugged at the door, it wouldn't open. I would try to open it from the outside, but to no avail. It would take a lot of coaxing and pleading to get him to let her out of the bathroom. I'm sure he saw this as great fun, but my friend saw it otherwise.

He was also quite fond of hiding my car keys. I would always set them on top of the stereo cabinet right by the front door. If I went to leave, they would be gone. I'd dig through my purse, and literally tear the house apart trying to find them. Finally I'd announce out loud that I was going into the bedroom for five minutes and when I came out my keys better be back where I'd left them. Sure enough, I'd come out of my bedroom and my keys would be on top of the stereo. I'd grab them and say "Thank you," through gritted teeth as I walked out the door.

On one occasion, this spirit saved our lives. In the middle of the night during the winter I woke up to someone shaking me violently. There was no one in the room except my husband, who was sound asleep. The house seemed very cold, so I got out of bed to check the thermostat. The temperature in the house was down below fifty degrees, and a strong smell of heating oil lingered in the air.

I woke up my husband who checked the furnace and said it wasn't working. We telephoned a twenty-four hour repair service and they immediately sent someone out. The repairman, after examining the furnace, announced that the furnace was shot, and it was a good thing I woke up because the house was in danger of catching fire because of the leaking heating oil. We gathered up the children, who were quite little, and went to a hotel. As we left the house I quietly thanked him for saving our lives. The next day we had a new furnace installed.

Other than the first floor, the third floor was the most active. It was occupied, for as long as I can remember, by a ghost I named Nathaniel. He'd watched me constantly when I was a child, and continued this when my husband and I moved into the house.

Although he'd never leave the third floor, there were times, when I was sitting in the dining room, that I swear I'd see his fingers wrap around the wall by the staircase and his eyes peering at me from around the corner.

When my son got older, I would hear him talking to someone in his room. I'd go upstairs and ask him who he was talking to. He'd tell me he was talking to his "friend," but that his friend would disappear when I came into the room because he didn't want me to get mad.

My husband decided to hang some shelves in my son's room to hold his ever-accumulating collection of toys. I told him not to hang the shelves next to the window because Nathaniel liked to stand there and look outside. Not believing in the existence of ghosts, my husband hung the shelves by the window. That weekend we went out of town to visit relatives. No one but us had a key to our house.

When we arrived home, I took my son up to bed and discovered that the shelves had been ripped from the wall and thrown around the room. There were gaping holes in the wall where the molly bolts had held the shelves securely in the studs. Yet my son's toys, which had been on the shelves, were neatly arranged on the floor across the room.

I called my husband upstairs to view the carnage. The next day he re-hung the shelves in the spot I'd originally told him too. No further incident of that type ever occurred again.

Because we had small children, I became concerned about Nathaniel being upstairs in the baby's rooms. I called in a parapsychologist friend of mine, and he brought a woman with him who had the ability to talk to Nathaniel.

She claimed that Nathaniel used to live in the house on the corner that was torn down to make way for a gas station. He moved into the upstairs of this house at that time. He told her that he lived in the middle 1800s and was severely mentally retarded in life. At that time, it wasn't uncommon for mentally retarded people to be kept in an attic, or locked away from society.

He said he knew he was dead, but was afraid to cross to the other side for fear of being ridiculed in death, as he'd been while alive. He said he loved the children and would never dream of hurting them in any way, and was happy for the company.

After the parapsychologist and this woman left, I started to think about Nathaniel's predicament and urged him to go into the light, that once he did, he would be freed from the handicap that plagued him in life. Eventually, Nathaniel left.

On the day we moved from that house, I was making one last sweep through to make sure the movers didn't forget anything. I was walking around the upstairs, and ended up in my daughter's room. She'd forgotten to take her favorite stuffed animal, Other Bunny, and it was lying on the floor. I picked it up and when I turned around I felt Nathaniel filling up the doorway.

Tentatively I said, "Nathaniel?"

In my mind, I heard him thank me for making him go into the light, and that he was extremely happy. He'd just come to say good-bye and wish me well. Then he left, and I was alone once again.

The people who bought our house only stayed for about a year. They've retained the house as a rental property. Every year, like clockwork, the tenants move out the day their lease expires.

Chapter Nine

Too Good Not to Include

While neither Linda nor I have been deeply involved with most of the events detailed in the following short stories, we felt they were too interesting not to be included.

Not Quite Ready to Retire

Strange things are happening after hours in a small store located in Southern Oakland County.

Several men who, on different occasions, were working late heard footsteps walking through the office. Thinking one of their co-workers returned to work for some reason, they'd go see who it was and find no one else in the building. This happened with such frequency they reported it to their boss who scoffed it off as over-active imaginations.

One night, however, their boss changed his mind. He was working late in preparation for the grand opening taking place the next morning.

The hour had grown late, and he decided to take a short break. He went into the bathroom to splash some cold water on his face and freshen up. While standing in front of the mirror drying his face, someone, or something, pushed him from behind against the sink. Before he could recover from the shock, he was spun around and pushed against a wall.

Frantic, he rushed out of the bathroom and back to his office. Quickly gathering his personal belongings, he ran out of the building to the safety of his car and went home.

Morrow Road—Truth or Myth?

The story behind Morrow Road is that a woman went outside in the middle of the night to find her toddler who, somehow, managed to get out of the house. Being winter, and quite cold, they both froze to death.

Some people say that if you go to a certain bridge on this road, you will see the woman, wearing a blood soaked white dress carrying her dead child. People have also reported being chased away from Morrow Road by a green light that comes right at them. Others have reported hearing a baby crying late at night, and the feeling of being constantly watched from the woods, or seeing dark figures walking down the street and no one being there when they investigate.

This story may or may not be true. Linda and I visited the site several times without seeing anything. I have to admit, it's quite creepy out there. On one visit I did feel as though we were being watched from the woods and Linda did manage to photograph a few orbs.

The orbs along Morrow Road.

If you ask around town, you will hear different stories about Morrow Road. One person told me that Morrow Road used to be the big "make out" place for teenagers. The people along that road became so sick of the traffic that they made up the story to keep the young people away.

This might be the case, but logic would dictate that if you tell a teenager a story like that, they would be more inclined to go there.

A cursory search of the vital records do reveal several mothers and their children dying in that area, but it's impossible to draw any conclusions from that information.

At the time this incident allegedly happened, scarlet fever, and other deadly diseases of the time were running rampant.

Truth or fiction? That's up to you to decide. No one really knows for sure. But one thing is for certain; Morrow Road will continue to draw the curious and those out for a thrill.

Linda and I anticipate Morrow Road will be one of the great urban legends of this area for years to come.

The Roseville House

Before Linda and her husband bought their current home, they lived in a Roseville, Michigan, home for about ten years. During that time, they experienced not only a lot of poltergeist activity, but also one bone chilling experience.

Before they bought it, the home was part of an estate, and had been owned by an older woman. Things went along fine for Linda and her husband for a while. Then one day Linda was in the house when she heard a noise coming from the kitchen. When she went to investigate, all the kitchen cupboards were open and the pots and pans strewn across the floor. She saw someone out of the corner of her eye, but when she whirled around, there was no one there.

On another occasion she went to the basement to do laundry. She noticed something on the concrete wall across the room. When she went for a closer look at it, she realized it was her name protruding out of the cement.

Linda became quite alarmed and went got a hammer to beat it off, but it wouldn't budge. She called to her husband who also saw it, and covered that part of the wall with a piece of plywood. Every now and then, Lisa would peek behind the wood to see if the name was still there and it was.

Several years later, before moving out of the house, Linda removed the piece of plywood to see if her name was still there. Not only was her name there, and Linda was shocked to see that the name of her youngest daughter was also there.

At this point, she became furious and quite scared. She picked up a small piece of metal off the floor and said, "I'm tired of those names being on the wall and I am not afraid of you." She started to scrape at the names with the piece of metal and, as she did, the names turned to powder and fell to the floor.

Armada House

The owner of a farmhouse in Armada told us about the strange happenings at the house they just moved into. The owner's brother and sister-in-law were over one day visiting. That evening, they decided to go for a walk out by the big old barn on the property. As they walked toward the barn, they saw a little girl run from the barn screaming and crying out. She ran toward the road, then back to the barn, and disappeared. The couple ran and got a camera and when they took a picture, in the light of the flash, they saw a man from the shoulders down, standing in the doorway of the barn wearing a white/beige shirt, black slacks, and suspenders. They took another picture and the man was still there. Eventually he too faded away into nothingness.

Linda, being told about the story, went to the home to investigate. Every time she tried to take pictures in the barn, the camera wouldn't work. She tried to use the owner's camera also, and it still wouldn't work, but when the owner of the house took the camera, it would take the picture. The owner took many pictures in the barn, some of which are included in this book.

Since this strange incident, the owner states that she has tried to communicate with the spirits in the house several times. One time she succeeded. The owner

An entity hanging out in the barn.

states that, although she was lying in bed wide-awake, when she asked the spirits to come talk to her, she had a vision of herself sitting in her kitchen. The kitchen became filled with the spirits of a family.

An orb outside the door to the barn.

A little boy spirit who looked to be approximately eight years old approached her. He was holding the hand of his little sister. He introduced himself as Mark, and his sister as Sarah, who was three years old.

Standing behind Mark, the owner saw an older boy. Mark introduced him as his brother, Jimmy, who was fourteen years old.

Behind Jimmy stood their parents, Abel, who was forty-four, and Sarah, their mother, who was thirty-four, and holding a baby named Janet, who was four months old.

The owner asked Mark what happened to everyone. Mark told her that some of them had died from pleurisy, and the rest had perished in a fire. The owner states that the next thing she remembered was waking up in bed the next morning.

Did she dream the whole incident? It's surely possible, but highly unlikely.

The owner also reports that when her son was a baby, they would hear a baby cry. When they went to check on their baby, the baby would be sound asleep. They report still hearing a baby cry now and then, even though there is no longer a baby in the house. They also report the sound of children running up and down the stairs.

They also report seeing men standing in the kitchen and living room at different times.

The owner reports someone calling "Mom," but it isn't her children doing it. Everyone in the house has reported items such as tools, books, etc., missing from time to time and then turning up in very strange places.

On several different occasions the owners say they smell a musty odor that lingered in the air, then would vanish as quickly as it appeared.

The scariest thing to them is that sometimes at night their bed will shake violently for no apparent reason, sometimes waking them out of a sound sleep.

The Town of New Baltimore

In the 1800s Anchor Bay was a much different place than it is today – especially the town of New Baltimore.

Imagine a bustling shipping port with large docks extending out into Anchor Bay. Moored at those piers are regal three-masted merchant clipper ships loading and unloading their wares. Stately hotels dot the downtown area as well as saloons, brothels, stores, and churches. In the distance you might hear the whistle of a locomotive as it roars into the station. There are people everywhere.

That is how New Baltimore once was. Now it's a quiet community filled with hard-working, friendly people. A beautiful park and beach have taken the place of the docks. The hotels are long gone, burned to the ground in the great fire of 1870. The saloons and brothels have fallen by the wayside, giving way to antique stores and other businesses.

While the landscape has changed, there are ghostly reminders of what once stood.

Our research shows a virtual feast of paranormal activity taking place in town.

Orbs outside the funeral home.

On Washington, the main street through town, stands the museum owned and operated by the Historical Society. This building was once a hotel, the only one that remains standing in New Baltimore. On the main floor are a common area, some displays, and the gift store. On the second floor are a research room, the curator's office, and other rooms displaying the museum's fabulous collection.

My first visit to the museum was the night of a holiday party hosted by the Historical Society.

After exchanging greetings, I decided to go upstairs to view the museum's holdings. When I got to the stair-

Mysterious ghostly things are going on at the Historical Society by night.

way I glanced up. At the top of the stairs I saw a man dressed in clothing from another era. One of the members of the Historical Society was with me and I asked him about the man as we walked up the stairs. After giving him a brief description of the gentleman I'd seen, I was shown a photo album. In that album I saw a picture of the man I'd seen at the top of the stairs and was told it was the man who owned the hotel. Evidently he's still around keeping a close eye on things.

In the research room I saw an elderly woman lying in a small bed. She appeared to be quite confused about all the comings and goings in her room.

A member of the Historical Society told me that after the hotel closed, it became a boarding house. Apparently this woman once occupied the research room.

The area around the Catholic church seems to be particularly active.

Orbs surrounding the statue of the Virgin Mary.

Outside the church stands a beautiful statue of Mary. Our pictures show an unusual number of orbs congregated around this statue. Could these orbs be the souls of the brazen sailors and fallen women looking for redemption? Or are they the founding fathers that built this town refusing to leave the place they loved so much? Or both?

We can't even begin to answer that question, but the fact remains they are there.

So next time you wander around town late at night and you think you're all alone, think again. For nowhere in the downtown area of New Baltimore are you truly alone.

The Haunted Rocker

No one knows for sure where it came from or who bought it, but the rocking chair has been in my family for generations. All I know for sure is that my Great Great Grandfather, Elias Scott Bacon died while sitting in that chair one winter afternoon.

I was sixteen when I first became aware the rocker was haunted. At that time the rocker sat proudly in my parent's living room, although no one was allowed to sit in it.

I was up in my bedroom studying, when my Mother called me downstairs. As I rounded the corner to enter

The haunted rocker.

the living room I heard a creaking sound and saw my Mother staring in disbelief in the direction of the chair. Following her gaze, I was amazed to see that the rocker was gently swaying. After a few minutes it stopped.

Periodically, mostly in the middle of the night, I would hear the squeaking of the rocker from the safety of my bed. Creeping down the stairs I'd peer into the living room and see it moving back and forth, always accompanied by the creaking sound.

The rocker now resides in the guest room of my home. Also in that room is the bedroom suite that once belonged to my Great Great Grandfather. My Mother told me when I placed the rocker there it was the first time since Elias Scott Bacon died that the rocker was reunited with the bedroom set.

The chair still rocks occasionally on its own. I hear it when I'm in my office writing. It really doesn't bother me, in fact, quite the opposite. I somehow find it comforting to know that the Great Great Grandfather I never knew in life has given me the opportunity to know him in death.

The Horsemen of Horse Grove

This story was authored by a friend of mine, Alice Bliss. Although it takes place in Iowa, it is simply too good not to include and I do so with her permission.

Just west of a small farming town in central Iowa stands twenty-two acres of trees and wetlands that are now part of a wildlife preserve. But long before either the Barnaby family or the Williams families ever came to the area, these gracious pieces of land had another name. This was the mysterious Horse Grove.

How this name originated isn't very clear to the local historians, but as a kid who has traversed all through the Grove and its wetlands, I would like to offer up some of my knowledge, observations, and speculations.

We'll start in a much better known portion of this piece of land, The Biological Reserve.

If you have ever wandered the trails between the actual park and the Iowa River, I'm sure that you have noticed the numerous trails that run like muddy creeks through these woods. Now some of them are much better marked than others.

Off of the beaten path, and up the hill and around the bend, you will come to a hole in the ground. On one side of this hole, you will notice that you can still see some of the bricks that one time made up the foundation of a house.

This is all that is left of The Barnaby house. The house was built by Elijah Barnaby around 1879, according to the city's records. But according to the town historian, Mr. Barnaby and his family only lived in the house for a couple of years. Apparently they moved into town around 1881. Although they gave no reason for the sudden change of heart, anyone that has camped in those woods at night can give you plenty of them.

I camped near the ruins of that old house one night, and I can tell you first hand that there are more than a few things haunting that area. I pitched my tent at four in the afternoon, and returned to it right about dusk. The first thing I noticed was the absolute silence. There were no crickets chirping or birds twittering. After ten or so, even the wind that had been blowing all day, seemed to avoid this place.

Around midnight, I heard what sounded like a wagon rumbling up the trail. Now common sense told me that there was no way a wagon with a team of horses hitched to it was going to make it through that narrow hiking trail! When I poked my head out of the little tent, I couldn't see anything and the noise seemed to rumble off into the distance.

No sooner had I climbed back into my tent than I heard music. It sounded like a fiddle player at one of those dances that were so often held around town at the turn of the century. The music lasted about ten minutes or so, but disappeared rather quickly when horses thundered through.

I looked out again, and sure enough, there were five men mounted on horseback racing through the park like they knew exactly where they were going. The strangest part though was that they didn't seem to disturb any of the low hanging branches or the tall grasses at the edge of the trail. And I know I saw one large branch pass right through them as they fled past me. That was my first encounter with the Horsemen of Horse Grove.

Had these been the creatures that had forced the Barnaby family to move into town all those years ago? My personal thoughts on that night were that yes, those eerie horsemen had been the cause of the family's exodus from the park.

Then there is what is known locally as the Glade. The Glade stands majestically between Reserve and the park. It's a wide-open field that at one side falls away into marshland. In one little corner of this field, there is a small area that had long ago been fenced in. Of course, today, you can only see the posts, if the grass hasn't gotten too tall, and you have to know what it is you are looking for.

In the middle of this fenced in area are five or six grave markers. These small, unassuming headstones bear no names, but if you look really close, you just barely make out the year, 1871. This place has gotten the name over the years as Campton's graveyard, but no one seems to know whom, if anyone, is buried there.

During the day, Campton's Graveyard is as peaceful as any cemetery, but I know of a couple people that have tried staying out there at night, and they will not tell anyone what happened out there.

A few years ago, the city council decided that they should dig up the graves and move them into the town cemetery. This project was plagued by trouble from the get-go. At first it was funding for such an undertaking. A local historian came to the rescue. Then it was finding the equipment needed. Another local company came to the rescue there. Since the owner of the tilling company lived on the very edge of the Reserve, he wouldn't have to find another way into the Glade. He could just bring the machinery across his back yard.

Then it was finding space in the new cemetery for the unnamed graves. That was solved when the town purchased more land from the farmer next to the cemetery. The family was proud to be helping out (although they were the only ones that profited from this venture).

Finding the grave markers was not difficult. Ask any kid that grew up in or around there and they can tell you where they are. Once the city had the equipment out there, that's when the real troubles started. First it was simple enough. The backhoe bogged down in the soft ground, the hydraulic line broke. Then the mayor tripped on a tangle of brush and broke his ankle. I clearly remember my dad saying right after the mayor's ankle was broken, that we shouldn't be messing with something that we don't understand.

When they finally got the backhoe fixed and the mayor to the doctor to have his ankle set, they began the digging. Now, please understand that it was already starting to get on towards nightfall and the crew only had a couple more hours to work.

That's when the screams started, very low at first. But they seemed to be coming closer with every foot of earth the huge backhoe removed. And just as the light of day started to fade, five mounted horses came bursting out of the park and raced towards the gathered townsfolk.

Although you could hear the thundering hooves, everyone knew that the soft ground would have absorbed the sound. Many fled as the horsemen raced past us. My family included, I might add.

As far as I know, the backhoe is still out there. I don't think the guy ever went out to get it. He died a couple of years later of a heart attack at the age of twenty-eight.

The city never did move the unknown bodies buried in the Glade. To the best of my knowledge, those poor unrecognized souls are still lying at rest in that place. I won't say they are at peace, because, judging from what I saw that evening, I don't think they are.

That's when the rumors started flying around that the grave markers show us the final resting place of the Horsemen of Horse Grove.

But who are the Horsemen? That question has plagued this small town almost from the beginning of its existence.

There are several theories, of course. There always are when an area has something it can't explain.

The best known and most widely accepted is that the horsemen are part of the posse that chased the outlaw Jessie James through the woods, but the time line just doesn't add up there.

Although Jessie James was still living in 1881, there is no record of him ever being as far north as central Iowa. And there is nothing to indicate that James and his band had anything to do with the Horsemen. And the James gang robbed trains and banks. There wasn't much they would gain from this town, even in 1881.

The other accepted theory is that the Horsemen were actually hunters and traders that had come through this area much earlier, and somehow they met their end at the Glade.

Okay, but that still does not explain the troubles you might find in the Reserve. The Reserve started out as a tax break for the a local family, but since then many people have found out that it too is the domain of the Horsemen.

The Hillman family has lived on the edge of the Reserve for a number of years, and although both are gone now, I was able to talk to them on several occasions about the odd things that went on at night right in their own backyard.

Old Man Hillman, as he was always called (I never even knew his first name until the day of his funeral), told me one time that he had encountered the Horsemen on more than one occasion. It was always right after dark and they never appeared to see him, they just thundered through like they were being chased by something. He even had to move his hog house because it was in the path of the Horsemen's flight and Hillman said that every time they rode through, several pigs would be found dead in the morning.

Apparently, the Hillman's survived out there by accommodating the Horsemen.

Mrs. Hillman never left clothes on the line at night, because in the morning they would be gone, only to turn up in the field torn to shreds. Old Man Hillman moved his hog house and they ended up getting rid of the chickens, because every time the Horsemen came through, the chickens would end up missing. They too would be found later, dead and many times without feathers.

The house that the Hillmans lived in is now gone and the road has been closed. The old wooden bridge has been taken out and the Artesian Creek has been forced to find another way to get to the Iowa River. Now it winds it's way through Horse Grove and joins the river at the end of the Glade.

Is that the end of the story of the Horsemen of Horse Grove? I don't think so. I know from talking to people that live there that the Horsemen still ride through the area. It's just that now, they are left to pursue or be pursued by whatever they have been riding from for all these years..

No one goes into the Reserve anymore. Even the DNR leaves the place alone. The Barnaby family has nothing to do with the Glade, and only the deer and the birds have to worry about what else might be running through the park with them. And they aren't complaining.

Chapter Ten

A Strange Thing Happened On the Way To...

While researching the stories contained in this book, many unusual and sometimes frightening things happened to me. Since I couldn't attribute these events to any one particular investigation, I decided to include them here, and have divided them into individual short sub-sections.

The Wolf

When I first started the investigation into the house on the hill, I had the vision of a large gray wolf lying on the stairway landing of my house. This vision gave me quite a start, because I wasn't sure if it was a friendly wolf or not. After a little research, I found that a wolf is a sign on protection, and is definitely a good thing to have hanging around the house.

This wolf, however, sometimes shows up other places when I least expect it. On several occasions he's shown up either in the passenger seat or backseat of my car. Sometimes he appears at the haunted locations Linda and I are investigating. He stands in front of me with teeth barred if a spirit or ghost is in the room.

My own dog, a Golden Retriever named Sasha, even saw him a few times. When the wolf was in my house he either appeared under my desk at my feet, or on the landing of the staircase going upstairs. Sasha would bark a couple times, then settle down and just watch him carefully. If the wolf got up and walked around the house, Sasha would track him with her eyes, but never approached him.

Recently I had to put Sasha to sleep due to an illness. When I returned from the veterinarian's office, the gray wolf was sitting by the door when I walked in the house. It was almost as if he came to comfort me. He remained close to me for about an hour before taking his leave.

My cats are also aware of his presence and give him a very wide berth whenever he is here. The wolf has never made any attempt to attack any of my animals. To go one step further, he seems totally disinterested in them.

I have to honestly say I have no rational explanation for his presence around me, but have to admit I feel considerably safer whenever the wolf is around, and hope he continues to visit often.

The Man Who Smokes A Pipe

Almost every time I'm on my way to or from Linda's house, I smell pipe tobacco coming from the backseat of my car. There is no smoke visible, but the tobacco odor is unmistakable; it's Cherry Blend tobacco. The only reason I know the particular tobacco is that I spent two hours in a tobacco store one day smelling all the different blends until I found the right one.

If I'm on my way to Linda's house, which is about four miles away, I will first notice the aroma when I pass Oakwood Cemetery, located a mile away from my house. When I get about a mile away from Linda's, the smell disappears. On my way home I will smell it just as I pull out of her driveway, and it will disappear as I pass Oakwood Cemetery.

The obvious conclusion is that this occurrence is associated with Oakwood Cemetery; however, it's impossible to say for sure. Could it be a spirit just out for a ride? I doubt it. Linda, and other people I know, go by the cemetery every day and have never reported anything similar happening to them. So for some reason I've been singled out to give this unseen hitchhiker a lift to wherever he's going.

At first I wanted to connect this pipe-smoking man to the paranormal phenomena at Linda's house. The first time I noticed him was on my way back from there. Then, when he started accompanying me to her house and back home again, that dispelled that theory.

I've tried several times to communicate with him, but so far he's been unresponsive. He's just content to sit in the backseat and smoke his pipe.

What strikes me as odd is that it's very rare for me not to sense the presence of a spirit or ghost as soon as it gets anywhere near me. Yet I'm unable to pick him up at all until I catch my first whiff of smoke, then I become acutely aware of his presence.

My impression of him is that he was a distinguished man in life, and quite a gentleman. I get the image of an older man, perhaps in his late fifties or early sixties, in an expensive three-piece suit. He always wears a matching vest and an ascot. I also feel he carries a cane. Judging by the style of clothing, it would be fair to say he lived sometime in the early 1900s.

I also get the impression that his hair is mostly gray with a touch of black. His moustache is neatly waxed and his grooming is impeccable. He is somewhat portly, but definitely a man of class and breeding.

As it is with the wolf, he doesn't show up all the time and the pattern is inconsistent. I've tried to take note of his comings and goings, and cannot associate them with any particular day or time.

Thinking his appearance might have something to do with the activity I'm undertaking that particular day, I've kept a journal. So far, there's no correlation between my activities and his.

He is showing up less frequently and I miss him in a way. When he did ride with me, I'd talk to him and tell him about my day. Passing motorists must have thought I was nuts talking to myself, but I feel rather smug knowing I have a kindly man riding in my car, puffing contentedly on his pipe, and enjoying the scenery as we travel down the road.

I've Just Been Disconnected

It seems as though a certain spirit or ghost doesn't want me talking on the telephone about this book. Every time I'm on the phone discussing the book, the phone will disconnect. Sometimes the line becomes so filled with static you can't hear. At other times a loud buzzing sound is heard.

Generally I'm "allowed" a half-hour or forty-five minutes before something happens. Its gotten to the point that I warn whoever I'm talking to that its going to happen and I will call them back on my cell phone. My cell phone seems to be immune to this activity. Thinking this was being caused by my telephone, I've tried putting in a fresh battery, but the problem persists.

Giving up on old telephone altogether, I bought a new one, and am still having the same problem. Funny how experience is still a great teacher.

At first, people didn't believe me and would scoff it off; until it happened when I was talking to them. When the phone does disconnect or fill with static, any attempt to use it for up to an hour is futile. During that hour's time, if I pick up the phone the static or buzzing sound will be there.

I think I've narrowed down the ghost causing this activity, but can't be sure. It appears that every time this phenomenon occurs, I'm talking about James Hatheway, from the house on the hill, or the house itself.

Can it be he's still trying to protect the family's privacy after all these years? Considering the secrets that, in James' mind at least, remain buried deep in the bowels of that house, it's not only possible; it's highly probable.

If indeed it is James Hatheway, his behavior, while disruptive, is probably one of his most endearing qualities. While not a pleasant man in life, it appears that in death he has found his sense of humor.

The Watcher

Ever since I started working on this book, there's been someone standing behind me reading over my shoulder.

As of this time, I haven't been able to discern who it is, or why they are so interested in watching me write. Let's face it, sitting and watching someone type is about as much fun as watching grass grow. Yet, he or she persists, and seems quite fascinated by my activity.

Is it possible that one of the ghosts or spirits has followed me home or is curious about what I'm going to write about it? The thought that a spirit has this ability is certainly intriguing and not out of the question.

When this first occurred, I thought it was the spirit of my father, but now I think it might be the ghost of James Hatheway. For some strange reason, it appears that James and I have forged some type of bond. He's always the first one to greet me when I visit the house, and I sense he's glad to see me. If you consider he's had virtually no one to communicate with for over a hundred years until I came along, it's not out of the question.

Most of the time it doesn't bother me, but sometimes the presence becomes so overwhelming it seems to fill the entire room. When this happens I announce to no one in particular that it's time for a break and go do something else around the house. Upon returning to my desk, I find the presence has abated, and continue my work, only to have it return a few minutes later. How does it know?

The only obvious solution is that it's watching, waiting, always there, but elusive. Every once in a while I'll catch a small movement out of the corner of my eye, but when I turn around, no one is there.

To make matters worse, sometimes I find myself talking to it: asking its opinion, discussing critical points in the story, etc. Not that I ever get an answer, mind you, but I figure as long as it's there, I might as well acknowledge its presence.

I've decided my only recourse is to accept that it's just always going to be there and to make the best of the situation.

Attack!

I can honestly say that these two events, which occurred in July of 2003, are the scariest I've ever experienced.

It all started around midnight. The sound of the dog barking woke me up. Since Sasha wasn't a big barker, I got out of bed to see what the fuss was about. Sasha was lying in the foyer barking at the front door.

I peeked out the window by the door, but no one was on the front stoop. I went to the door that leads to the backyard and turned on the floodlight. There was nothing in the backyard. Satisfied that nothing was amiss, I went back to bed.

Not even two minutes later, I heard the murmur of a man's voice. I couldn't make out what he was saying, except when he said my name.

At first I thought it was my husband telling me that the dog wanted to go out. I rolled over onto my stomach and was just about ready to tell him she didn't when I felt a leg on the back of my legs, then I felt a body on top of me. It took me a second to realize that this wasn't my husband.

My eyes flew open and I saw my husband peacefully sleeping to my left. Whatever was on top of me, virtually pinning me to the bed came from the right.

I tried to move, but couldn't. I opened my mouth to scream, but no sound came out. The more I struggled against this unseen force, the tighter its grip became.

Having no other recourse, I began to recite the Lord's Prayer and ask God to help me. Within seconds, the presence released me. Panicked, I leapt from the bed, raced into the den at the end of the hall, and collapsed into a chair.

My hands were shaking so badly, it took three attempts before I was able to light a cigarette. Just as I began to calm down, I heard footsteps coming down the hall from the direction of the bedroom. Assuming it was my husband checking to see if I was okay, I looked down the hallway, but saw no one, yet the steps were getting closer.

It was then that I sensed a very strong presence coming towards me. I could feel him standing there staring at me. My breath was coming in short gasps. How do you fight something you can only feel, but not see?

Sasha started to bark. Her ears were back and her teeth barred. I saw her watch him as he moved away from me and out the front door.

The next similar event came a mere three days later.

The alarm sounded as usual with the familiar voice of talk radio jarring me awake.

My husband got out of bed to get ready for work. I turned over to go back to sleep. A few minutes later, I heard a male and female voice talking. I caught bits of the conversation, but wasn't paying much attention.

Since the alarm was on the other side of the bed, I was lying there with my eyes closed debating on whether it was worth the effort to turn it off.

A minute or so later, I felt someone breathing in my ear. It didn't register at first, but when it did, I opened my eyes and realized two things. First, the radio wasn't on, and second, I wasn't alone in bed.

I jumped up and ran into the hallway. I yelled for my husband, but realized he'd already left for work. Reaching around the corner, I turned on the light in the bedroom. Naturally, no one was in the bed, but I still felt a lingering presence in the room.

Some people might say both events were just nightmares, but they'd be wrong. I was wide-awake when both attacks occurred.

Nothing like this ever took place before, or since, and I don't have a rational explanation for what happened. What bothers me most is that whoever, or whatever, it was called me by name.

At first I thought it was the same being that watches over my shoulder while I write, but no. The entity that attacked me both times was a menacing presence. You could feel the anger and vindictiveness in the room.

The spirit or ghost that looks over my shoulder while I write is not threatening. He is more of a kindly soul.

When these attacks took place, I contemplated what could have triggered them. There was nothing in my personal life that could have caused them, so that left me with what projects I was working on at the time. There were two: the Mills house and the house on the hill.

Since I'd been working on the hill house investigation for some time prior to the attacks I can't attribute this incident to that particular place, but it hasn't been eliminated. As for the Mills house, I'd felt nothing particularly threatening while in the home, but can't eliminate it as a possibility.

It's been well over a year since these attacks took place and I'm not any closer to knowing what caused them, and who, or what, made them. But, I figure as long as they don't happen again, I'm ahead of the game.

Conclusion

We hope you've enjoyed the haunting little tales contained in this book. We've sure had fun researching and writing it. If you have any true ghostly tales you'd like to share with us, we'd welcome the opportunity to talk with you. Please e-mail Debi Chestnut at ghostmist6@ yahoo.com or ghostwriter246@hotmail.com. If you don't have access to e-mail you may reach us through our publisher at the following address. Debi Chestnut or Linda Sparkman, c/o Schiffer Publishing Ltd., 4880 Lower Valley Road, Atglen, PA 19310. Of course, all personal information will remain confidential.

So until next time remember, when you're home alone late at night and something goes bump in the night, or you see something move out of the corner of your eye, you really aren't alone. Happy Hauntings!

Animal Spells and Magick

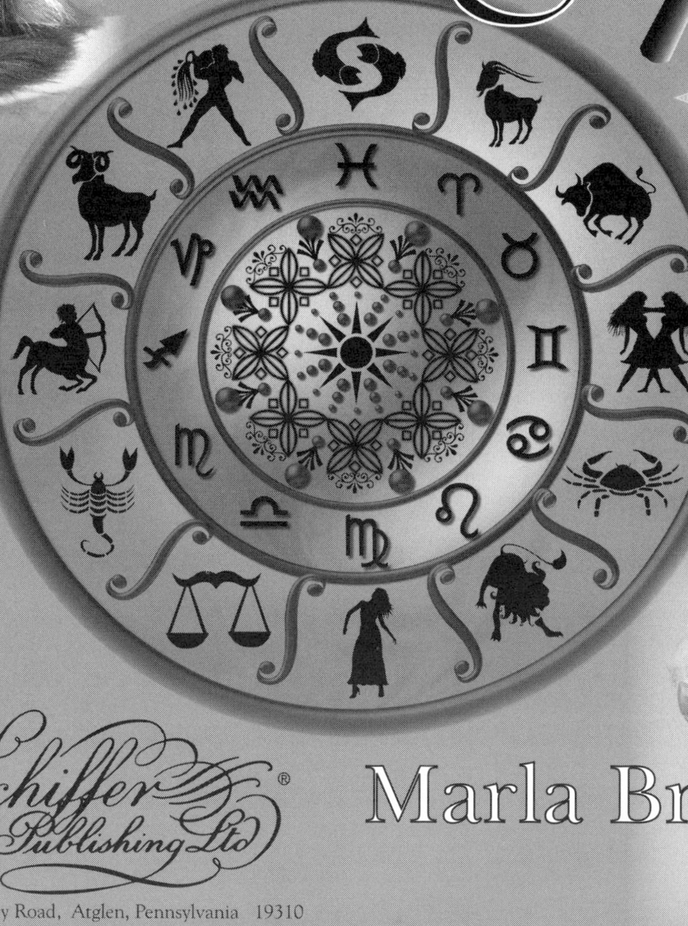

Schiffer Publishing Ltd®

Marla Brooks

4880 Lower Valley Road, Atglen, Pennsylvania 19310

Photo and Poem of Rainbow Bridge courtesy of RainbowBridge.com.

Spells and advice in this book ares not intended to replace veterinarian care or as treatment for any particular problem associated with animals. The intention is to spend more quality time learning about your pets, directing your positive intentions towards them and learning how your interactions with them can bring you closer to nature and the world of animals. Use information at your own risk.

Schiffer Books are available at special discounts for bulk purchases for sales promotions or premiums. Special editions, including personalized covers, corporate imprints, and excerpts can be created in large quantities for special needs. For more information contact the publisher:

Published by Schiffer Publishing Ltd.
4880 Lower Valley Road
Atglen, PA 19310
Phone: (610) 593-1777; Fax: (610) 593-2002
E-mail: Info@schifferbooks.com

For the largest selection of fine reference books on this and related subjects,
please visit our web site at **www.schifferbooks.com**
We are always looking for people to write books on new and related subjects.
If you have an idea for a book please contact us at the above address.

This book may be purchased from the publisher.
Include $5.00 for shipping.
Please try your bookstore first.
You may write for a free catalog.

In Europe, Schiffer books are distributed by
Bushwood Books
6 Marksbury Ave.
Kew Gardens
Surrey TW9 4JF England
Phone: 44 (0) 20 8392-8585; Fax: 44 (0) 20 8392-9876
E-mail: info@bushwoodbooks.co.uk
Website: www.bushwoodbooks.co.uk

Some photos courtesy of Art Explosion.
Text and photos by author unless otherwise noted
Following photos courtesy of www.bigstockphotos.com. Incense© Stephane Benito, Healing stones© Katarina Bratkova, fresh herbs© Gordon Swanson, Rat with a candle©Dmitry Maslov, Wiccan objects©N Joy Neish, sweet dreams©Lisa Turay, Golden Chinese Dragon statue©Ralf Kraft, Yellow tang©Mark Aplet, American Cocker Spaniel©Tammy McAllister, scratching fleas©Pattie Steib, Dog Heaven 1©Leslie Murray, Paradise in Sky©Alexey Lashin, InLove©Christiane Cornelius, Quill on Parchment©Sandra Caldwell, Parchment©Dana Rothstein, Braided Horsetail©Trijnie Duut; jar of stuff©Andrew Smith, Lavender Candle and Flower Display©Lijuan Guo, Newborn Black and White Kitten©Alexey Ukhov, Hermatite©Martin Novak, Fluffy Clouds 03©Elana Bennett, Green Leaf©Mike Selvar, meditation©Olga Brovina, Tibetan Singing Bowl©Ana Coates, Horseshoe02©Heinz Waha, Sachet©Sampford Peverell, Light Point (Flair)©ktsdesign, Bottles with essential oils©Elena Schweitzer, small kitten©Birute Vijeikiene, Tree trunk: I think I'm lost© Nikola Spasenoski, Dandelion with floating seeds©Paul Lampard, pet rat eating©Duncan Noakes, Blue-eyed dog©Jennifer Walz, kitten under a book©Anna Schram, magic©jadedme, venus statue©p. lange, witches kitchen©Anna Schram, wiccan tools©N Joy Neish, zodiac©Viacheslav Sevast'yanov, Astrology symbol©Petra Roeder, Totem Pole©pr2is, Pentagram©jörg röse-oberreich, Bronze statuette of fun cat isolated over white©Aleksandr Kurganov, Halloween cat©Daniel Loncarevic.

Library of Congress Control Number: 2010935688

Designed by Mark David Bowyer
Type set in UniversityRoman BT / New Baskerville BT

ISBN: ISBN: 978-0-7643-3626-3
Printed in the United States of America